CREATE YOUR OWN WORKOUT PROGRAMME.

First of all I would like to **thank you** for your trust.

I would also like to mention that my idea with this book is to share my experience, opinion and knowledge with you about what I realised is the most adapted, efficient and enjoyable way to train for me and for my clients.

I am a Personal Trainer but first of all I am passionate about sport and physical activity. I have always been interested to know how the best athletes train, eat and sleep to maximise their potential.

Sport has always been in my life, since a young age. But I decided to make health, fitness and wellbeing a priority for me in 2020. And I also decided to help people that would like to do the same. By training them, sharing what I learnt with them and with you, through this book.

Even though I am a Personal Trainer, and sport is my job, I consider myself as the average person who wants to look after its health and improve but also someone who wants to enjoy other things.

I practice weight lifting because it helps me find mental peace and physical wellbeing. However I also want to keep time for the other things I love.

If this sounds like you, you are in the perfect place. I am deeply convinced that this book will help you lots. Its goal is to make you autonomous and give you all the tools you need to make your own workout programme that will allow you to develop yourself physically and mentally.

Please, I'd love to hear what you think about my work. Feel free to share your opinion through a review on the platform where you got the book from, share this book with friends or even contact me.

@equilibriumworkout

equilibriumworkout.com

Hope you enjoy reading it,

Jeremy.

Create your Own Workout Programme.

COPYRIGHTS.

Copyright © Jeremy Grilo, 2024.

All rights reserved.

CONTENTS.

There are some important rules and knowledge you need to know in order to build the best workout programme for you. I organised them into different chapters.

1. Patterns over muscles.
2. Choose the right split.
3. Full body.
4. Keep it short and intense!
5. 4 indispensable things to implement in every single programme.
6. Progressive overload and deload.
7. Do cardio! And separate it from your strength training?
8. The importance of periodisation.
9. Optimise your nutrition: the 80-20% rule.
10. Sleep well and drink enough water.
11. Preparation is key.
12. Less is better than nothing.
13. Stick to the basics and use compound movements.
14. Do not overthink it!
15. How to make sure you improve.
16. Workout templates.
17. Exercises bank.
18. Advice and tips to make the most of this book.
19. Thanks.
20. Acknowledgements.

Create your Own Workout Programme.

1. PATTERNS OVER MUSCLES.

Have you ever heard about the rule that says you need between 10 and 20 sets per week and per muscle group to stimulate your muscles enough to improve? And have you ever tried it?

It works, don't get me wrong, but I find it hardly sustainable in the long term.

There are about 600 muscles in the human body, can you imagine how long it would take you every week to get your 10 to 20 sets per muscle group? A lot of time! And to be completely honest, I think if I had the time to spend on it, I still would not want to do it. And I do love sport.

I gave it a try, and it did not work for me. I felt overwhelmed by the amount of exercises and sets I had to perform for each session. It became a new source of anxiety for me. I would count every single rep and set I performed to make sure I have had enough and I was reaching the amount needed. I would feel a knot in my stomach before going to the gym, as I would be scared to fail, and sport would just become one more source of stress in my life. And I'm sure you'd agree on that one, it is absolutely not the goal. Actually it's completely the opposite!

For the regular human being, fitting 3 strength training sessions per week is a real challenge.

Life is extremely busy with a lots of things to handle such as work, kids, time, motivation, family and friends, other social life or other physical activity, plus private worries to deal with and so on. An endless list.

I believe that wanting to work every single muscle in an old school style is realistic if you have time, patience and body building is your first priority.

However I know as a fact that you do not need to work out that way in order to improve, get stronger and healthier, and stay fit in the long term.

Instead, organising your sessions around patterns of movement makes much more sense! I find it much more fun, convenient, fast and less stressful!

Your body counts 6 important patterns of movements:

- **Squat (single or double leg):**

It is performed in a standing position and the goal is to bring the hips as close as possible to the ground in a vertical movement, keeping the core vertical too. It includes 3 flexions: one on the hips, one on the knees and a dorsiflexion on the ankles. It targets the quads and the glutes.

Flexion: decreasing the angle between the bones of the limb at a joint.

Dorsiflexion: movement of the foot toward the shin.

Ex: back squat.

- **Hinge (single or double leg):**

The core is moving forwards but do not go further than 90 degrees. The hips remain horizontal and can move backward. They can move down vertically but without breaking the angle of 45 degree flexion. Hinge is performed in standing position and the goal is to move the core towards the horizontal plane. Through flexion in the hips and knees to balance the weight. No ankle dorsiflexion is achieved. It targets the hamstrings, glutes and hip extensors.

Ex: deadlift.

- **Push (single or double arm):**

Horizontal: it consists of moving the resistance away from the chest in a horizontal plane. Your arms are then pushing at (more or less) 90 degrees with your core that remains stable and straight. The main muscles involved are chest, front deltoids and triceps.

Ex: push ups.

Vertical: you are moving the resistance above your head or at least into a vertical direction based on your core. You are pushing away from your shoulders. The muscles mostly involved in this movement are front and lateral deltoids, triceps and rear deltoids too.

Ex: military press.

- **Pull (single or double arm):**

Horizontal: the resistance is moving towards you as you are driving your elbows on a horizontal plane behind you. Your arms move at 90 degrees from your core. Muscles involved are latissimus dorsi, lower traps, rhomboids and rear deltoids.

Ex: rowing.

Vertical: the resistance is moving towards you from up to down or from down to up on a vertical plane. You are either driving your elbows down, parallel to your core, or up parallel to your core too. Muscles mainly involved are latissimus dorsi, trapezius, rear deltoids and biceps.

Ex: pull ups.

- **Loaded carries:**

Performing walking for a predetermined time or distance with a weighted implement. It can be carried overhead, on your shoulders, with arms straight or a mix of those. Often, upper body is more challenged with back muscles being more involved. But the legs work too.

Ex: farmer walk.

- **Core:**

(Anti) Extension:

You want to resist overextension of the lumbar spine. Meaning you need to keep a neutral spine position and stop your spine and back to overextend (arching).

Ex: front plank.

(Anti) Lateral flexion:

You are trying to resist flexing from the side. Meaning you need to keep a neutral spine position and try to stop your spine and back to flex to one side, and then to the other. It is a great exercise for lateral stability. Note that it needs to be performed on both sides of the body.

Ex: side plank.

(Anti) Rotation:

You want to resist a horizontal force placed on your core and coming from one side. Trying to keep your spine in neutral position you stop your core from twisting to one side. It helps muscles strengthen and stabilise by placing asymmetrical and unbalanced forces on the core. Note that it needs to be performed on both sides of the body.

Ex: pallof press.

Hips flexion:

Keeping your spine in a neutral position, you want to work on your core strength by using a hip flexion meaning reducing the angle between your hips and your thighs. It is a good way to develop your core and your hip flexors by flexing them.

Ex: stand up knee raise.

When you know and understand these body functions and patterns, developing 6 patterns of movements sounds easier and more accessible than working on 600 muscles, right? The thing is through these 6 pattern you actually work and involve your entire body!

Is it optimal?

The answer will vary depending on people. I believe the right programme is the programme you can do. The right programme is adapted to your goal, needs, level and limitation. But also to your lifestyle, not the opposite! You also need to enjoy it and be able to perform it on the long term! You can have the most optimal program in the world, it will be useless if you do not use it!

Using patterns rather than a muscles split, as long as you use (mostly) compounds movements, and perform enough sets, will give you results!

Obviously this has to come with consistency and an appropriate lifestyle (nutrition, hydration and sleep) but we will talk about that in the next chapters.

2. CHOOSE THE RIGHT SPLIT.

As I said above, fitting 3 strength training sessions a week is a big challenge for most people. Sticking to it is difficult too.

However you now know that using patterns will save you time and make your sessions more fun. Now the next step is to pick up the right split that works for you.

What is a split?

Every programme is divided into sessions. Depending on how many times per week you want to train you will divide your programme into a specific number of sessions. There must be an overarching organisation to that, as you need to make sure all the patterns of movement are covered. The way you will divide the patterns into your sessions is called a "split."

When you are about to choose the right split for you, you must answer the following questions:

      a. What is my goal?
      b. How many times per week do I want to train?
      c. How much time do have I for each training session?

What is my goal?

First of all, I'd like to say that no matter your goal, working your entire body is a must! Your body is a machine with interconnections. Meaning that having a strong upper body and a weak lower body makes no sense. The opposite doesn't make sense either, as they work together and for each other.

If you work out for health reasons, that is even more true. You can't give up on a specific body part because you do not like it, or it is too hard.

It is important to mention that there is no mandatory exercise, only mandatory patterns. If you do not like back squat then do not do it. Do one of the numerous variations that exist.

When it comes about how many exercises per pattern you need to perform, it all depends on your goal. As I just said, I always recommend to work your entire body however I understand, from experience, that most people have specific goals. If it is not about losing belly fat, which is probably the most common of them, it'd be about a specific body part. If that is the case for you it is something to take into consideration.

If you are a runner, meaning it is your favourite and main activity, you might want to use strength training to enhance your physical performances and reach your Personal Best on your race. In that case you'd probably work your legs more, in different conditions and be careful not to gain too much weight on your upper body. It might be different if you are a swimmer or if you practice golf. In these cases strength training is a side activity that has the goal to improve your performance in your main sport. It is then important to be more specific about these areas and body parts that you want to develop. As much as what exactly you'd like to improve (strength, explosiveness, power and so on).

How many times per week do I want to train?

In my opinion, training less than twice a week won't give you much results. By that I mean significant results that you can feel and see. Training once a week is better than nothing, it will give you a feeling of wellbeing and satisfaction, and probably a good sweat. But this is not enough to challenge your body and make it create adaptations.

We now know that it is better to hit a body part twice a week rather than once. You want to train enough but you don't want to train too much either. The amount of training you will fit in your week is important to know to make sure you split your training the best way possible and find the right balance, between enough stress and not too much, placed on your body.

I have met lots of people that decide to get into strength training and give it their all. They'd train 4 to 5 times a week and realise after a few weeks that it is too tiring for them, takes them too much time, is too difficult mentally etc. I always recommend to start with something you think is sustainable in the long term. To me, 2 sessions per week sounds like something doable for most people. Two sessions of an hour each is probably an amount of time that even the busiest people can be free to train.

Training twice a week is a good way to start. You can still increase this number, whenever (if ever) you feel like it. Even for a short period of time. However I believe that once you have decided how many times you'll train, it is important to stick to it as a minimum. Make a promise to yourself and do not train less than what you decided.

How much time do I have for each training session?

This is a tricky one. That is where reality and expectations meet. Ideally we want to be as efficient as possible and maximise the time spent to train and have the best results possible. There is a thin line where these 2 worlds meet. You'd have to align your goal, with your availability and the reality.

Let's say you'd like to learn a new language and dedicate some time to it. You are now studying twice a week, for 10 minutes. Would you expect becoming bilingual within the year? Probably not. There is nothing wrong about studying for 10 minutes twice a week, but this is not aligned with your goal. Also, you'd not expect amazing results by doing that and the exact same logic applies to strength training.

Including a warm up, I'd recommend at least 45 to 60 mins of exercise per session. Less can happen every now and then but it can't be enough, in my opinion, to build great results in the long term. There is a lot you can do in an hour if you are serious about it. Meaning not checking your phone, being strict on the rest and having a plan (a well-designed programme)!

If you come prepared, have the right intention and are serious, you can do a lot within 60 minutes. And if you really think about it, spending 2 hours of the 168 you have available every week to train is not much! Having more energy, releasing stress, being physically and mentally healthier for only 2 hours every week sounds like the best investment ever to me!

When you come to this final step it is important to remember that overall, you want to create a programme that you will sustain in the long term! As I just said, there is absolutely no point to start training 5 times a week, just to end up with only 1 or 2 sessions after a few weeks.

Your training sessions need to fit into your life and not the opposite. This is a crucial idea to keep in mind when you are picking up the split that will do it. You're better off starting slowly and then increasing the amount of sessions, if you have more time/energy to dedicate to it. Or even have an extra session to do on a lighter week that leaves you with more free time to exercise.

Here are different splits that I find very practical, for most people:

Push/pull/legs:

As you can probably guess, you'll spend one session pushing, one session pulling and one session working on your legs. It is interesting when you want to train 3 times a week but can also be tricky if you are not sure you can do 3 times. If you miss one of the sessions there will be one body part you won't train at all.

Upper/lower/full body:

One session is dedicated to your upper body, one to the lower body and the last one will be full body. I really like this way to train. However you have to be sure you'll train 3 times or you might end up with one session for each muscle group instead of 2 and so don't optimise the benefits.

Upper/lower:

Alternating upper and lower sessions is a good split as you make sure you have enough rest between sessions on the same body part. It seems great if you train 4 times a week and not ideal if you do less. If you don't hit the gym 4 times, you won't be sure to have hit all body parts twice in the week and doing legs once, and upper once, is not the best approach in my opinion.

Split body parts:

Training only one group of muscles at every session will make sure you get a lot of exercises in. It sounds great for people that train 5 times and plus per week. However this style of training seems to be outdated to me. Unless you'd like to be a body builder, this is most probably not the right split for you.

Full body:

In my humble opinion, full body is the smartest way to train for most people. It has plenty of benefits and I highly recommend people to train that way. I use this split with 95% of my clients and for myself. Let me explain you why.

3. FULL BODY.

If your time to train is limited and you want to make the most of your workout then full body is the best option for you.

In fact, using a full body template has all the following benefits:

- It enhances your physical development.
- It allows you to adapt your weekly trainings to your life.
- It is time efficient in and around your sessions.
- Full body but not only.

It enhances your physical development.

Nowadays it is well known that working muscles 2 to 3 times a week is more efficient than doing it only once. We also know that there is not really a point to doing it more than 3 times a week, especially for hypertrophy (the increase in the volume of an organ or tissue due to the enlargement of its component cells).

When you put your muscles under the right amount of positive stress (meaning that can have a positive effect on your body), which could be done with weights, elastic bands or even your body weight, you push your body to create adaptations in order to be able to face the same stress anytime soon. To do so, your body will get stronger by increasing the size and the density of your muscles, tendons etc.

This being said, there is an important thing to keep in mind: you lose everything you do not work on. It sounds tough but it is sadly true.

However, it is also nuanced. The longer you train (over the years) and the more consistent you are, the more chances you have to keep your gains on the long term.

If you have been training for years, have been very regular to the gym by hitting it 2 to 3 times a week or more then it is very unlikely that you'd lose all of your accomplishments.

For an experienced weightlifter, studies say that it can take up to 9 weeks to see a significant decrease in physical conditions and abilities. A good thing to keep in mind.

Knowing that, it then makes sense to use full body trainings. It will allow you to put your muscles under stress 2 to 3 times a week, keeping in mind that it is when they are at rest that they recover and build their strength.

Burning more calories.

When you practice full body workouts, using movement patterns, you are burning more calories than for a regular muscles split.

First of all, you are using your legs. And some of their muscles (quads and gluteus) are the biggest on your body and so they require more energy when they are being used. Leg exercises strongly engage your core too, which is good because core is often forgotten and not put under enough stress.

Also, studies show that leg strength exercises can stimulate the release of large amount of hormones, including cortisol, testosterone and human growth hormones (HGH). Cortisol makes your body better at responding stress and increases fat metabolism. Testosterone helps in the repair of damaged muscles and HGH promotes muscles growth, boosts your immunity and fat metabolism.

It adapts your weekly trainings to your life.

In a perfect world you would train as planned every week. The gym would never be busy and you would never wait for any equipment. You would implement progressive overload (chapter 6) and keep on lifting more and more every week at every session.

We both know that the perfect life does not exist. Life requires us to be adaptable. And that is perfectly fine. Adaptation is a key of success.

When you use a full body program, you have choice. You can hit the gym 2, 3 or even 4 times a week without impairing your development too much.

In fact, when you use methods such as push/pull/legs, or a body parts split, if you ever miss one of the sessions you planned you might feel unbalanced. If that repeats, you would also probably keep on missing the same session every week. Most probably the one you like the least and therefore probably need the most. Something that would not happen with full body.

Let's say your current program has 3 sessions per week. You perform the first one, it goes great, then the second one, awesome. But something comes across the 3rd one. Tiredness, lack of motivation or life duties and number 3 can't be done.

Sadly you are not doing full body and you end up with your push and pull sessions done, but nothing for your legs. Or just back/biceps and shoulders/legs but no work for your chest and triceps. Does it make sense?

Let's say the same thing happens but you are using the full body method. You still missed one session and completed only 2, but you have hit all your movement patterns twice this week! This will enhance your muscle growth and ensure that you have worked on all the muscles of your body.

It is time efficient.

Full body is not only work efficient but also time efficient. In fact it allows you to use supersets, no matter your level.

What is a superset? It means performing 2 exercises back to back with no or little rest in between.

There are other methods that can allow you to use them too but they do not include, in my opinion, all the benefits that full body provide (as mentioned earlier).

If your level allows it, you can even use tri sets (3 exercises back to back) or giant sets (more than 3).

Let's say you are doing supersets. It'd go as follows:

Session B	1a. push V	1b. pull H SA	2a. push H SA	2b. pull V	3a. core	3b. carry
Sets	3-4	3-4	3-4	3-4	2-3	2-3
Reps	6-12	6-12	6-12	6-12	12-20 or time	Time or distance
Rest	45s	1m30	45s	1m30	45s	1m30

You'd then perform 6 exercises, in less time than if you were not using supersets, and without impairing your performances as you are not working the same muscles back to back (or very few of them). You also perform a fair amount of sets and reps during your week.

What else do you need?!

Full body but not only.

Using full body and compound movements does not mean you can't use other intensifications (training strategy designed to push a muscle past failure) or isolation work (exercise that involves only one joint).

If you have more time, or want to emphasise a specific muscle, you can then add some extra exercises that will isolate it/them. You can see in the example above that biceps are being worked on. You can add one more exercise at the end of the same programme, or you can also twist it around and do tri sets, or giant sets, or even remove some sets, to add more exercises or change your resting time etc.

There are countless options that can vary upon the time, depending on your current goal and availability. Keeping in mind that a minimum is needed to keep improving, or maintaining your muscle mass.

Different types of intensification.

Here are a few intensifications that I find interesting enough to use for me or my clients.

The pyramid.

You increase the weight over the sets but decrease the reps. Once you reach your maximum, or the number of sets you decided to perform, you go the other way around. You decrease the weight over the sets and increase the reps to come back to the number of reps performed on the first set.

Pre-fatigue.

With this intensification you perform one isolation exercise and move on without rest to a compound movement including the same muscle that you isolated. This is a good way to emphasise it and give it more stress but make sure you are not reaching failure on the first exercise. I find it meaningful if you struggle to target a specific muscle. For example you find it difficult to feel your chest on a chest press, before your set, perform a set of triceps extension. They will then be tired and you won't be able to use them that much on your bench press. Your chest will then take over.

Drop set.

When you reach failure on one exercise, drop the weight and keep performing more reps until your reach failure again. Repeat it and repeat it again.

Forced rep.

This needs to be performed with your PT/gym partner. When you are about to reach failure you'll ask for help to complete the very last rep, the one you can't complete. No help should be needed on the eccentric phase but only the concentric one. (Read more about concentric and eccentric in the next chapter).

Negative reps.

In this case, only the eccentric phase is performed during all the sets (or only at the end of a regular set, if you'd like to). You might need your PT/gym partner to help you with it depending on the exercise performed. Note that if you are performing a full set of negative reps, you can increase the weight you'd use for normal reps (with concentric and eccentric phases) by up to 20%, as the average person is 20% stronger on eccentric phases. You can also slower the eccentric phase, spend more time under tension and so make it more challenging.

Pause rep.

This consists of taking a short rest after you performed the last rep of your set, and performing as many reps as possible. Before doing the same thing again and again. You keep the same weight all the way long.

Keep in mind that intensification techniques are best used by advanced-level people, in order to not impair the good form of each movement. Also, they should not be used all the time and for each set, but only every now and then, to add a difference stress to the muscles and push until failure.

I consider them fun to use, and I like to do it every now and then, however I do not overestimate their impact. As I will explain later in this book, there are principles that are much more important when it comes to training and improvement.

Create your Own Workout Programme.

4. KEEP IT SHORT AND INTENSE.

I know how much life is demanding. We all have work, family and social duties. We also have different things to handle and different things to work on. And fitting in 3 strength trainings per week is a real challenge (which is worth it in my opinion).

Also, knowing that you will work out for 1 hr 30 or more can feel overwhelming or even bring you motivation level down, just thinking about the amount of exercises and time you will have to spend!

My best advice for you is to keep it short! 60 to 75min of strength training (including warm up and cool down) 3 times a week is enough!

Keeping workout sessions short saves you time and energy. Especially mentally. I love to think that with only 3 hrs per week of dedication and hard work, I am looking after my body, my physical health and my mental peace.

If you are using supersets (as mentioned above) you will be able to perform a fair amount of sets per week for each pattern while keeping your training short enough to free up time outside of the gym.

Also, the total amount of time spent in the gym does not matter. It does not make any difference, but efficiency does. And time under tension does too.

Here are 2 very important things you need to keep in mind.

    a. Reps, time and sets are just ways to calculate time under tension, meaning the time that you put stress on your muscles, tendons etc.
    b. Weights are only tools to apply stress. It could also be your own body weight, as much as a chair or whatever else.

Time under tension and positive stress are two important variables to understand. Depending on the time and the stress you apply to your body, the response created by it changes. And so different muscles fibres are targeted, and different adaptations occur.

Important notions to understand.

Time under tension.

This is the total amount of time that a muscle or group of muscles endure mechanical stress, during resistance exercise.

Ex: if you do a set of 8 reps with a tempo of 3 seconds of eccentric and 1 sec of concentric then the TUT (Time Under Tension) for one rep is 4 secs. So 32 secs in total for the set.

Positive stress.

As explained before, your body creates adaptations to become stronger when it is put under a specific positive stress, meaning a stress that can have a positive impact on your body.

It can be applied by any type of equipment, the goal being to challenge the body enough to make it understand that it needs to be ready to answer the same amount of stress anytime soon. To do so, the body will create adaptations, and get stronger by increasing the size of the muscle fibres and mitochondria.

By applying the right amount of stress you make your body more resilient. It is important to find the right quantity of stress that will send the signal to your body to develop, making sure you are not applying too much stress and are risking a potential injury.

Mechanical stress.

This can be referred as 'outside in', meaning the conversion of mechanical energy into chemical signal and adaptation. If you perform reps with a weight/load for a specific time, you are putting your body, and this targeted muscle, into a mechanical stress.

Ex: barbell back squat, dumbbell bicep curl etc.

Metabolic stress.

This can be referred as 'inside out'. The metabolism, is the chemical processes going on within a living organism to maintain life. The chemical process to break down carbs, fats and proteins and turn it into energy is known as metabolism.

Concentric phase.

When the muscle is shortening.

Ex: on a back squat, your quads are shortening when you stand back up. That is the concentric phase.

Eccentric.

When the muscle is lengthening.

Ex: on a back squat, your quads are lengthening when you go down, this is the eccentric phase. The average person is 20% stronger on this phase (for any movement). Which makes tempo very interesting and important when it comes to programming.

The tempo is the pace you are performing a movement at. If you perform a squat and use a tempo of 1-5-1-1, it means that will take 5 seconds to perform the eccentric phase. Any other part of the movement will be performed within 1 second.

Isometric.

There is no noticeable change in length in the muscle. It is a static movement.

Ex: you sit against a wall, with your knees at 90 degrees and hold the position for as long as you can. There is no change in length in your muscles but you are still working them.

Repetitions range.

The range of repetitions is important because it will implement a specific stress on your body and create a specific adaptation. Select it depending on your specific goal for this exercise, and for your programme in general.

Keep in mind that when you choose a range of repetitions you have to pick a load that will allow you to stay in that range. If you feel you could do more reps than the range chosen, increase the load. Over the weeks you want to stay into the same range but increase the challenge and so the load.

Also, the resting time is important. If you do not rest enough or if you rest too much, it will impact the stress implemented on your muscles, and so the adaptation. I cannot recommend you enough to have a watch with you when you exercise, and to pay attention to your recovery times.

Create your Own Workout Programme.

Goal	Strength & power	Hypertrophy	Muscular endurance	Plyometric & jumps
Sets	3-5	3-4	2-3	3-6
Reps	3-6	6-12	12-20	4-6
Rest	2 to 5 minutes	90sec to 2 minutes	90sec to 2minutes	30 to 45 seconds

5. 4 INDISPENSABLE TO IMPLEMENT IN EVERY SINGLE PROGRAMME.

Warm up.

Obviously as a PT I always recommend to warm up properly, for 10 to 15 minutes. Using light stretching, mobility, compound movements and light cardio to make sure your joints, muscles and heart are already. Consider this warm up as the very first exercise of your session.

No matter the number of sets you are performing per exercise, I'd also recommend to use the first one to keep warming up (using a lighter weight, with the same number of reps you are targeting).

Not everyone has 1 hr30 to 2 hrs to work out 3 times a week. If you do and find that it works better for you, that's fair enough, do it. Otherwise if you are like me and want to optimise your sessions (learn more about that later in Chapter 9), short and intense workouts will probably work better for you.

We could argue over whether not everyone has 60 to 75 minutes to exercise 3 times a week, as well. And we could probably find people for whom that is true.

However, I'd say that everything depends on priorities. If you make your health one of your top ones, I'm deeply convinced that you can make room for it. And that hopefully this guide will help you optimise the time you dedicate to yourself and to your current and future health.

First things first, I highly recommend you to get some gentle movement in at the very start of your warm up.

Move the following in all the directions possible. Flexion/extension/rotation/abduction/adduction/bending etc.

- Neck.
- Spine.
- Shoulders.
- Hips.

In my experience they are very sensitive parts of the human body and require some specific attention.

Secondly, I'd recommend you to perform some compound movements, with no or very little weight. Kneeling push ups, squats, walking lunges, hand walks etc.

Thirdly, raise your heart rate. Jumping squats, jumping jacks, high knees, jumping rope, there are plenty of exercises to ramp up your heart beat.

And finally, perform the patterns you'll use during the upcoming session, with light weights, and slowly increase that to the weight you are planning to use during the session.

I usually allow 15 minutes to do this, which is, in my opinion, enough to get yourself ready without being too tired before starting. In terms of intensity, I'm targeting 6 to 7 out of 10.

Failure.

Muscle failure.

When the neuromuscular system can't produce enough force to overcome a specific workload, or when a muscle can no longer contract concentrically

This is an important one, and possibly the most important of all the rules. If you want to create adaptation, and challenge your body enough, you have to get close to failure, if not, going to failure. It is not recommended to go to failure at every set, of every session. However being 2 to 3 reps from failure will make a difference.

When you get to failure your nervous system works a lot, it is also mentally very demanding. What I tend to do, when I programme for myself or my clients, is build up the reps gradually over the weeks, until failure on the last week of the program.

If the program is meant to last 4 weeks, I'd work in the chosen range of reps over the first 3 weeks and go to failure on every set or on the last set of each exercise for the very last sessions of the program. By doing that, the body is challenged every week, if the weight is chosen accordingly, to respect the range of reps selected, until it is completely ready to go to failure on the very last week.

Everyone is different and you need to learn what works for you, however it is certain that you have to find the right balance between challenging yourself enough, and not too much.

Planes of motion.

When programming your sessions you need to keep in mind that not only patterns of movement are important, but also planes of motion. Make sure you are exploring all the motions within you different programmes.

There are 3 you have to pay attention to:

- **Front**: dividing the body into front and back halves. Any movement parallel to this line is known as frontal.

Ex: lateral raises.

- **Sagittal**: dividing the body into left and right halves using an imaginary line gives us the sagittal plane. Any movement parallel to this line is known as sagittal.

Ex: lunges.

- **Transverse**: divides the body into superior and inferior halves. Any movement parallel to this line is known as transverse.

Ex: core twist.

Plyometric and jumps.

Plyometric.

To exert maximum force within a short interval of time. Any activity that targets fast-twitch muscle fibres. Fibres that help generate explosive power that increase speed and jumping height.

The time of contact with the surface you're pushing off from, must be less than 1 second, to be considered as plyometric, which is the main difference with jumps.

Implementing plyometric and jumping in your training is a great way to keep on developing your fast twitch muscle fibres and an opportunity to make your trainings more fun.

If you are training for your daily life, meaning to feel good and ready to face everyday challenges, it is very beneficial to work on these muscle fibres.

It's also perfect if you are doing strength training in order to complement another sport. Most sports require explosiveness, and implementing this type of stress is a great way to transfer your gains from the gym, to any other activity you might be doing.

Plyometric and jumps are often forgotten or overlooked in programmes but are essential in my opinion. They bring fun, variety and a different stress, which is useful in many different aspects of your life.

6. PROGRESSIVE OVERLOAD/ DELOAD.

What is progressive overload?

You might know it already but in short, progressive overload means to keep on challenging your body, to push it to keep on creating adaptations. This overload can result in being able to lift more weight, do more reps, more sets, more sessions, and have less resting time.

To create the perfect workout, you first need to have a goal. You then need to decide how many times you will train and find the right split. Once you've shaped the frame of your programme you will select the range of reps, depending on this goal. You will finally pick up the exercises. For the selected ranges of reps, you'd then pick up a weight that allows you to perform them, keeping 2 to 3 reps in reserve (away from failure). And this step is crucial as you need to select the right weight. Getting something too light would not create enough adaptation and getting something too heavy could lead you to an injury.

We know that the human body needs, in theory, 4 to 6 weeks of the same exercises to create enough adaptation and so to keep on improving. Less than 4 weeks is not enough to force it to create the specific adaptations needed, and more than 6 weeks could potentially lead you to plateau or boredom.

What I usually do, for myself or for my clients (they both vary for technical reasons), is building a programme that would last 4 to 5 weeks.

The first week is about finding the right weights for each exercise selected as previously mentioned. Weeks 2, 3 and potentially 4 are used to incorporate progressive overload and improve technique and form for every single exercise.

There are different range of repetitions: 5-8, 8-12, 12-15 and 15-18+. It then makes sense to start your new programme at the lowest number and add one more rep every week (keeping in mind that progression is not linear and that actual life often comes up, with business, tiredness, worries, lack of sleep and recovery etc).

By the 4th or 5th week, we can give our max effort week. This is where I'd push myself and my clients to reach failure on every single exercise! A very intense week, that is safe to perform after having developed skills, form and technique for 3 to 4 weeks before on these exercises. Be aware that this will be a very intense and tiring week for your nervous system. I can't recommend enough to drink water, eat and sleep well and allow enough recovery between sessions.

After this max effort week, I'd then move on to a new programme with the same principles. The first week will be used to pick up the right weights. I'd also ask people or myself to take it easier on this week. It'd give time to the body and the brain to learn new movements but also get some active recovery after the max effort week. This week would be considered as the week 1 of the new programme but also the deload week from the programme before. Note that exercises can vary over the course of a programme. They would never completely change, but some variations could be implemented to suit the person better or to work slightly differently. Also, be aware that you do not have to change all the exercises from a programme to another one. I'd tend to keep some of them. Usually to improve their form or if someone has a specific goal regarding a specific movement.

What is a deload?

A deload is a period used to give rest to your nervous system but also your brain. Progressive overload is physically tiring and also mentally challenging. Having to push and do more every week has its limits. And it is better to anticipate it rather than fixing it later. Use this deload week to lift less. You can lift less weight (for example for the exercises that you kept from your previous program), or do less reps than your plan for this new programme, or just less sets.

Use this week as a recharge and an active recovery from your previous programme, but also as a preparation for the following one.

For myself, I'd use programmes that last 4 to 5 weeks (depending on the month) because I find it more motivating to start a new month and a new programme at the same time.

Also, I love variety. Changing my programme often allows me to incorporate exercises I have never done before and try them out. Or initiate a new focus, that could be back strength, or more legs exercises or working on explosiveness.

This is completely up to you. You do not have to change it all from one month to the next, but can do it. You can also change focus, or not. Try this out and find what works the best for you.

7. DO CARDIO! AND SEPARATE IT FROM YOUR STRENGTH TRAINING?

I can't recommend you enough to do some cardio. Strength training is very good to build muscles, strengthen your joints, slow down your aging process etc. However the 'outside' part of fitness is not the only one that matters. The 'inside' is at least as important. Let me explain it further.

Some people would argue that lifting weights is already cardio, and I cannot deny it. However when you are weight lifting, cardio is not your main focus. It is just a side effect of the exercises you are doing. Managing and controlling your breath when you lift is very important and can enhance your performance, however I think it is important to spend 1 or 2 sessions a week developing your cardiac functions.

In my opinion, a 20 minutes light walk on a treadmill is not enough. You're probably walking every day, and that is a good thing (for your heart functions and metabolism), but you want to stress your heart, lungs and all your respiratory system in numerous different ways and at different levels.

Create your Own Workout Programme.

How do heart rate zones work?

Zone	Intensity	% of Heart Rate Max	Benefits
Zone 1	**Very light**: you are able to keep going forever.	50-60% Anaerobic*.	Boost recovery. Warm you up. Burning fat zone.
Zone 2	**Light**: you can go for a very long time and keep talking.	60-70% Anaerobic.	Improve general endurance.
Zone 3	**Moderate**: heart rate is going higher and you struggle to talk.	70-80% Anaerobic.	Improve blood circulation.
Zone 4	**Hard**: unable to talk, all your focus goes to what you are doing.	80-90% Aerobic*.	Improve speed endurance. Carbohydrates being used mostly. Increase ability to handle lactic acid.
Zone 5	**Maximum**: you are giving it all!	90-100% Aerobic.	Blood and respiratory system work at their max.

Anaerobic*: your body requires immediate energy. It relies on stored energy sources rather than oxygen. Any activity that breaks down glucose to use it as main energy.

Aerobic*: use of oxygen as main energy in order to meet physical demand.

I would not say that any one of these 5 zones is more important than the other. I'd encourage everyone to vary their training and switch to organise their cardio around these 5 zones. They all have their specificities and benefits and they are all interesting to use and develop.

However as zone 1 is something you can practice outside of the gym (walking or cycling to go to work, weekend walks etc) I'd not include it your programme. I'd usually focus on zones 2, 3, 4 and 5 and probably alternate them and switch them up from month to month.

If you are looking for developing all the aspects of your fitness, and like to vary your trainings, as I said previously, I'd recommend to change your workout every month (4 to 5 weeks) to keep it fresh and engaging. If you do so you better organise everything in advance and implement periodisation (to see in the next chapter).

Should you separate cardio from strength training?

This might be a disappointing answer but, it depends. There is no universal rule and no one answer to this question.

You want to avoid the interference effect. What is that? Simply that if you are performing cardio and strength on the same day/training session, they might interfere with each other and you would not get the best results possible for each of them.

There are different point of view on this, and they all have their pros and cons.

If you want to prioritise strength.
In that case, you better not do cardio on the same day. Some studies show that if you do not have a 6 hour window between your two sessions, you are diminishing your strength gain. Meaning that if you have enough time (more than 6 hours) to recover and rest between the two trainings, you can still do it. I'm assuming only a few people have this opportunity (athletes) and the general population is very unlikely to have enough time to train twice a day.

If you want to prioritise cardio.
In this situation, cardio will be your main focus, and strength training is supposed to help you perform better in that. An adapted strength training programme is required, with the right exercises and stress being applied. The same conclusion occurs to me, it is better to separate your strength from your cardio sessions.

The 'high-low' method.
Understand high and low intensity. This method, made famous by Charlie Francis, suggests that the intensity of your training is more important than the type of training you do. For him, you can practice high intensity cardio like sprints and high intensity strength training like powerlifting on the same day.

If you got enough rest before your low intensity day, there is no problem. You can then perform low intensity cardio, like tempo runs, and low intensity strength, like lifting techniques with low weights, in your next training session.

Barre in mind that your nervous system needs enough time to recover between hard sessions.

Benefits of using cardio to recover.
Low intensity cardio vascular workouts can help pump blood to damaged muscles, nourish them and fasten their recovery. In my opinion doing some cardio, at least once a week is a must. It does not have to be intense, it all depends on your goal, but training in zones 1 or 2 will help you recover faster, burn some fat and make your heart working. The ideal being to train in zones 3 or 4 too and be as complete as possible. If you do not have enough time, alternate them.

8. THE IMPORTANCE OF PERIODISATION.

'If you do not do periodization then you are not writing programs, you are writing workouts.' *(Cosgrove and Rasmussen – Secrets of successful program design).*

It says it all, if you do not have a mid to long term plan then you don't have a global vision of where you are going to.

What is periodisation.

Periodisation is the planned variation of training variables such as reps, sets and loads. I'd also include focuses (back, legs, etc) and the type of cardio you'd like to work on (zone 2 to 5).

For instance, when you train your cardiac system, depending the benefits you'd like to have (cf: tableau chapter 7), you will use the adapted zone.

It works the same for strength training. Depending on your goal you have to adapt the reps, sets and loads you will use. Keep in mind that these variable are only a tool to reach the goal you target.

For example, if you want to develop your power you will use a short reps range, a high number of sets and a heavy load. In this case, lifting heavy will develop your type 2 muscle fibres (cf. next section).

Periodisation is created backward, meaning you are starting by the final goal, where you want to be, at the time you want to be there, and create your program backward until the day you are starting.

Ex: if you want to lift 120kg on a barbell back squat in 6 months, you will set that as a goal and go through all the steps you need to reach before getting there. You will then set a goal to reach by the 5th month, and by the 4th month and so on. Including all the variations you will use, deciding the exercises, sets, reps that you will perform etc.

Keep in mind that periodisation and planification are both estimations. That is theory and in real life practice is a little bit different. You cannot predict how your body will exactly react to your plan. It might follow it perfectly or might not. You might have to adapt and change a few things along the way but planning is the best way to maximise your results. Optimise the probability to have the results you want at the time that you want too.

Muscle fibre types.

	Slow-Twitch Type 1	**Fast-Twitch Type 2A - Intermediate**	**Fast-Twitch Type 2B**
Activities	Long distance, endurance, low weight training.	Shorter efforts, strength, sprinting, jumping, powerlifting, higher weight training.	Shorter efforts, strength, sprinting, jumping, powerlifting, higher weight training.
Size	Small	Large	Large
Force production	Low	High	Very high
Fatigue	Slow	Quick	Very quick
Contraction speed	Slow	Quick	Very quick

Type 1 of muscles fibres are the smallest, but they are surrounded by more capillaries, which give them more resistance to fatigue, but also less ability to produce force.

Type 2A and 2B are larger in size but easier to fatigue. However they produce more force, in a quicker time. It is fair to say that type 2A is a mix between type 1 and 2B, and known as intermediate muscle fibres. Even though all muscles fibres are a mix of these 3 types (1, 2A and 2B).

Depending on your physical activity, your percentage of muscles fibres types vary. If you are doing long distance running, swimming or cycling, you probably have a higher Type 1 percentage. If you are doing heavy weight lifting, sprinting or jumping then your percentage of Type 2A and 2B is most likely to be higher.

It is also important to mention that the average person tends to be 50/50, however some people might naturally have more of one type of fibres, which gives them a natural pre-disposition to a specific activity. Often, being 'talented' for a sport, pushes you to practice it, which enhances your physical capacities even more. Champions are probably a mix of natural advantage and specific hard work.

Workout planning.

Planning your workouts months or at least weeks in advance makes it easy to make sure you are using all the tools you want and creating all the adaptations that you target.

As beginner, you better start building up some muscles, using a longer reps range before getting into heavier weights.

Otherwise, as far as I know, there is no specific order you need to use in your periodisation. As long as you are not an elite athlete, for whom, it'd be different depending on your competitions etc.

It is then up to you to decide when you'd like to focus on specific body parts, power or explosiveness for example.

Personally I like to mix everything up and always keep a bit of everything. My training would be probably composed of some heavy lifts, higher reps range exercises and some explosiveness exercises. And I'd alternate zone 2, 3 and 4 for the cardio.

However there would be some body part focuses and some type of training focuses too (power, explosiveness, mobility etc) depending on my mood, goal or fancy at any moment.

All these parameters are really up to you, and you can play with them around to avoid boredom and keep your trainings engaging and motivating for yourself or/and your clients.

Create your Own Workout Programme.

9. OPTIMISE YOUR NUTRITION: THE 80-20% RULE.

Nutrition is not really part of a workout programme, but it is linked to it and will have a massive impact on your ability to perform during your sessions. Nutrition is a factor that will make a difference!

The basics.

There are 3 main components to our diet: protein, carbs and fat. Each of them has its function, and matters. Here is an overlook of the main functions of these 3 important sources of energy.

Protein.

Protein works in chains of amino acids. There are 9 of these essential amino acids which are not produced by the human body and that you therefore need to get from your food. And there are 11 non-essential amino acids that your body creates.

Your body uses these amino acids to build and repair muscles and bones, and also as source of energy. Proteins also have other functions (such as acting as enzymes and hormones, maintaining proper fluid and acid base balance, providing nutrient transport or making antibodies.)

Having enough protein helps you maintain your muscle mass, as your body would use protein as fuel to provide energy when carbs and fat intake is inadequate.

It is recommended to consume 1.5 to 2 grams of protein per kg of body weight every day to ensure your stocks are full. For instance if you weight 70kg you should have between 105 and 140 grams of protein on a daily basis.

You find protein in poultry, meat, fish, eggs or lentils.

Carbs.

Carbohydrates provide your body with glucose that is converted to energy, used to support body functions and physical activity. They are sugar molecules broken down into glucose and used to fuel the body's cells, tissues and organs.

You find carbs in pasta, rice, grains, fruits or legumes.

Fat.

Fat is often seen as bad, but just like with protein and carbs, is essential to maintain good health. It helps give your body energy, protects your organs, support cells growth, keep cholesterol and blood pressure under control and helps your body absorbs vital nutrients.

You can find healthy fat in seeds, walnuts, nuts, fish or oil.

Calories intake.

In term of nutrition and diet, and as well as learning about protein, carbs and fat, having a clear understanding of how calories work is important.

At rest, when doing nothing but lying on your bed, your body burns calories. This is known as your Basal Metabolic Rate or Resting Metabolic Rate. On top of that, you also burn calories when you walk, cook, do gardening or daily movement. This is known as Total Daily Energy Expenditure.

If you eat more than what you burn, you gain weight. If you eat the same amount as what you burn, you maintain your weight, and if you eat less then you lose weight. It is then up to you to do some strength training or not and eat enough protein to build muscle and burn fat. Think of strength training as a way to shape your body. If you want to drop some weight and use a calorie deficit without training, you will lose weight but you will not get stronger. Developing your muscle mass is highly recommended no matter if you'd like to lose, maintain or gain weight.

The 80-20% rule.

Counting calories everyday can be very triggering for some people. I'd not recommend it on a long term, unless for specific extreme cases, but I'd recommend it on the short term, for a month. The average human being often eats the same ingredients, dishes and has the same drinks. If you can have a better idea about the amount of calories you eat every day, that could help you have a better control on your weight.

It is not easy, if not impossible, to eat 'healthy' all the time. Also restriction and starvation is something I always avoid for myself and for my clients, as it might lead to food binging. I also avoid using the term 'cheat meal' or 'cheat day' as to me, it stigmatises 'bad' food as much as it creates an obsession about it. I do not like the idea of 'starving' myself for a week to then allow myself 'cheating' on one day.

There is absolutely nothing wrong about wanting to eat some cheeseburgers, cakes or other processed food.

What matters to me is the amount of it that you will have. In my opinion, I think that eating unprocessed homemade dishes 80% of the time, along with well programmed workout is enough to maintain a good and healthy physique.

One more time, you do not need to count accurately the percentage of healthy and processed food you are having, but keeping this balance in mind, and trying to reflect it into your plate is good enough.

Other than food, there are 2 other factors that make a lot of sense to me in order to be healthy and enhance your mental and physical performances: sleep and water.

Create your Own Workout Programme.

10. SLEEP WELL AND DRINK ENOUGH WATER.

Sleep well.

There are numerous studies about sleep, and several books. And they more or less all come to the same conclusion. Sleep is crucial! No matter what time you go to bed and wake up, it is highly recommended to sleep at least 8 hrs per night.

Circadian rhythm.

A circadian rhythm is known as the sleep-wake pattern that occurs every 24 hrs. It is usually based on the day light and night darkness. We're are not all the same, however, and for this reason people have different sleep patterns.

New born do not have a circadian rhythm when they come to the world. They develop one over their first week and months, which explains the disrupted sleep they go through during the first days of their lives. As they grow, they adapt to the world and its light, as much as they start creating melatonin that will structure their sleep pattern.

It won't surprise anyone if I tell you that teenagers often go to bed quite late, and wake up very late too. It might be more surprising to learn this has absolutely nothing to do with laziness, but it is explained by their circadian rhythm at this stage of their lives.

Stages of sleep.

REM: Rapid Eye Movement.

REM sleep is when your brain activities are at their highest. Almost at the same level than when you are awake. This stage usually last 10 to 60 minutes, and does not occur for at least 90 minutes after you fell asleep. It is known as crucial for your brain memory, creativity and learning. This is when you are dreaming the most intensely.

During this stage your body experiences 'atonia' which means it is paralyzed. Except for your breathing system and your eyes, that move extremely fast from side to side. This allows your brain to completely fall into sleeping mode without being disturbed.

REM takes up about 25% of sleep for adults.

NREM: Non Rapid Eye Movement.

NREM is made up of 3 different stages.

The 1st one, or N1 is when you are falling asleep. This usually last 1 to 7 minutes and you are not yet deeply asleep, which means you can be woken up very easily. Your brain is slowing down and getting ready to be turned off. You are also going through uncontrolled movements as you are getting ready to step into stage 2.

N2 usually lasts 10 to 25 minutes and can get longer as the night goes on. In this stage your brain finally relaxes, and your muscles too. There is a drop in temperature of your body and your heart is beating slower as you are breathing slower too. Your eyes stop moving in this stage. N2 can represents up to 50% of adults nights.

Stage 3 or N3 lasts from 20 to 40 minutes and shortens during your night. Your breath slows down even more and that is the stage where you sleep the deepest. It is very difficult to wake from this phase, as this phase is important for recovery and growth. It is also crucial for brain creativity and memory.

This stage is very present in the first half of the night and then slowly gets overtaken by REM sleep.

Sleep cycles vary in length but usually last more or less 90 minutes, and are composed, of N1 leading to N2, then to N3 to end up in REM sleep, in that order. Once the cycle is finished, it all starts again (except for the Stage N1 as you do not fall asleep again during the night as you are already asleep) until you naturally wake up or get woken up by your alarm.

Melatonin.

Melatonin is a hormone created by the human body. It does not make you sleep but it sends the signal to your brain that it is time to sleep. It is only a trigger.

At night, with the darkness and based on your sleep pattern, circadian rhythm and sleep cycle, an increase of melatonin production tells your brain that bedtime has come. Have you ever experienced feeling tired in the evening, but staying awake, to then end up not able to sleep?

It is because you have missed your melatonin peak. In an opposite way, in the morning, as melatonin's production decreases, your brain understands that it is time to wake up.

Some people use melatonin supplementation when they struggle to fall asleep or are experiencing jet lag.

To conclude, we can tell that looking after your sleep is a very crucial part of training, but also in life in general. Having a good sleep pattern helps you memorise all the information that you came across during the day, getting rid of the unnecessary ones and keeping what matters. It also helps your body fully recover from all the activities you have been through, as well as learn the new movements you might have been trying.

It is highly advised to sleep 8 hrs per night and have a regular sleep pattern that will make you sleep and wake up every day at the same time. It can take up to 3 days for your brain to restore fully its functions after sleeping 7 hrs (and not 8 hrs) for 3 nights in a row (*Why we sleep – Matthew Walker*). This means that a weekend is not enough to allow your brain to perform at its best again. Keep in mind that you cannot catch up the hours you have lost. Once they are gone, they are gone.

The point of this section is not to scare you, or stress you, about the impact that a lack of sleep could have on your brain. But only to make you understand better how sleep works, and hopefully make you realise the importance to have a good sleep pattern. I do think that understanding things better rises people awareness, and has more meaning, that will result in more action.

Drink enough water.

You probably already know that 60% of your body is made of water. 75% of your brain and of your muscles is water too. Staying hydrated allows to regulate your body temperature, protects organs and tissues, lubricates joints, dissolves nutrients and minerals to make them accessible and much more.

Every day you are losing water through breathing, sweating, and urinating. You lose even more if you exercise or if temperatures are high

You get water from fluids but also from food.

In average, 20% of our daily water intake comes from nutrition. And the remaining 80%, which represents about 1.5L for women and 2L for men per day, comes from our drinks.

If it can sounds difficult to drink that much water every day, there are few tips that can help you.

Drinking water as soon as you wake up.

In fact, you spent the last 8 hrs without drinking so it makes sense that water should be your first thought in the morning. Starting with a full glass of water will help you replenish and start your day hydrated.

Carrying a bottle of water with you all day is also a good way to remind you to think about it. You can also give yourself targets and goals. For instance, drinking 2 glasses of water with each meal of your day would be a great way to help you reach your daily goal.

Muscle benefits.

As mentioned before, water is essential in the transport of nutrients and minerals through your body. Including the musculoskeletal system. It encourages muscle growth because it participates in the delivery of the material needed to construct glycogen structure. Having enough water insures that you have an appropriate electrolyte level, that your joints are lubricated enough and that you avoid cramps.

But water is not only important to perform, it also helps you to recover.

In fact, drinking water flushes toxins out of your body and helps with muscle soreness and tensions.

Mental benefits.

Did you know that dehydration is the main cause of headaches?

Next time you experience one, before taking any medicine, try to drink water and see how it goes. This might be why your head aches a bit in the morning. You have spent quite a lot of time without hydrating your body and so your brain.

Not consuming enough water can have severe impacts on your brain performance, such as inability to focus, fatigue and sleep issues.

It is well known that you can survive longer without eating rather than without drinking water.

The different types of water.

Water is essential to the human body and to your health. There are 5 types of water you need to be aware of:

- **Tap:** the water you can get from any tap, at home or in a restaurant. The easiest and fastest way to get water.
- **Mineral:** water from a mineral spring with a natural underground source protected from pollution. It contains at least 250 parts per million total dissolved solids. Which a real natural and not added (except for carbon dioxide). Mineral water is naturally filtered and has a steady composition.
- **Spring:** spring water is mineral water that can go under slightly more treatment, that doesn't' change its nature or qualities. Spring water contains less minerals than mineral water.
- **Distilled:** water boiled into vapour and condensed again into liquid in a separate container. The goal being to remove all impurities that are not boiling into the original container and so get rid of them. It is a type of purified water. It often does not contain some minerals, like calcium or magnesium, as well as contaminants.
- **Purified water:** water filtered through one of the following processes: reverse osmosis, distillation or deionization.

Reverse osmosis: use of semipermeable membrane to remove salt and impurities.
Distillation: boiling water and condense it again into a different container to remove minerals and impurities.
Deionization: removing salt and other mineral ion molecules.

Drinking enough water means keeping your electrolytes in the right balance, and in terms of electrolytes, the one you probably need the most is sodium.

When you sweat, you lose lots of sodium and so it is important, especially if the weather is hot, to replenish your body stores.

Sodium helps you prevent muscle cramps - but not only that.

It will also help your blood pressure regulation, your muscle function, your digestion and optimising your brain functions.

If you want to perform better when you are providing a long effort, adding a tea spoon of salt for a litre of water sounds like the right thing to do. Choose a salt that is mostly composed of sodium (sea salt for example).

The quality of the water you drink will highly impacts your hydration and recovery and you want to select the right type of water depending on what you need. Drinking a high quality water allows a better recovery and hydration.

Create your Own Workout Programme.

11. PREPARATION IS KEY.

Fail to prepare, prepare to fail. This is obviously not from me but it does make a lot of sense when it comes to programming. Also I do not like wasting time, and I'm sure you do not either. With a busy life and different responsibilities, optimisation is a key skill, and so is preparation. When it is time to write programmes for myself and for my clients, there are different elements I pay attention to.

Gym layout.

If I or any of my client is working out in a gym, or in a home gym, I always pay attention to the layout of it. You do not want to perform an exercise and then travel to the other side of the gym and perform a second exercise to then come back to the initial spot etc... Especially if you are using supersets or tri sets. Also gyms are often busy and you can't prevent anyone from jumping into your spot as soon as you leave it to go somewhere else.

When it comes to create your session, I'd highly recommend to associate exercises that you can perform easily back to back. I also pay attention not to use all the equipment of the gym. Make sure that what you want to use it close by.

For example:

1a. BB bench press.

1b. KB squats.

1c. Side plank.

You would not have to travel between these exercises and can use this time off to fully recover. You're saving energy and time.

Equipment.

Obviously if someone has a home gym with little equipment, I'd have to compose the programme with what they have. But if you are going to a commercial gym, there is probably plenty of different equipment you can use. If you want to save time and effort that is something you need to pay attention to. You can use different types of weights to make sure you are not travelling from one spot to the other one. Or you can actually do the opposite and use the same equipment, but adjust the weights on it. Another alternative is mixing up weights exercises and body weight exercises.

For example, a tri set can be as follow:

1a. Overhead barbell press.

1b. Single leg deadlift (using the same barbell but changing the weight on it).

1c. Front plank.

A good way to maximise space, equipment and time.

Mix up stances.

If you remember well, I have talked about patterns in the very 1st chapter. To me, they are more important than muscles. And for this reason you have to pay attention to stances. Split stances take more time to perform than regular stances (with 2 feet on the same line, or using both arms at the same time). One set of Bulgarian split squats, would definitely be longer than one set of goblet squats. For this reason I'd always mix stances up in my programmes. It would probably be a squat and a split stance hinge, or a hinge and a split stance squat. This will balance the time spent for these exercises within your different sessions.

For example:

1. Barbell squat.

2. SL deadlift.

Supersets.

As explained earlier in this book, supersets are a good way to save you time. Depending on your level, your goal, and how many sessions you are doing per week, there are different types of supersets you can use.

For example:

1. Opposite muscles/patterns.

Ex: pull ups/shoulders press.

2. Upper/lower.

Ex: push ups/squats.

3. Same body part/pattern.

Ex: barbell chest press/push ups.

Create your Own Workout Programme.

12. LESS IS BETTER THAN NOTHING.

If you are looking for to learn more about how to build your own workout programme, it is most likely that your health and wellbeing are one of your priorities, or that they are becoming one.

We all have different priorities, and in my case, their order changes from time to time. Work might take over on some periods, while sometimes holidays might take over. As a fitness professional, my health and therefore my trainings are always in the top 3. Depending on the week, on my schedule and obligations, I will train more or less. But I always make sure that I train at least 3 times a week. Because it is the minimum number that works for me. If I ever go on a weekend break, I'd make sure I keep aside 1 hr during my trip, to work out with some suspension trainer or any equipment I'd be able to bring with me. Or to run. Or to do some jumping rope. It is something that I think about before leaving, when preparing my trip, and that I do consider part of it.

As said previously in this book, the advantage of doing full body is that if you are missing one of your trainings, you still hit all of your body patterns at least once every week (in the case where you are training twice). Keep in mind that less is better than nothing. If you do not have time to do all the sets you wanted to, do less and include some intensification. If you do not have the usual equipment available, mix up the exercises but keep the same pattern of movement. If you can't work as heavy as you wanted to, lower your tempo. If your time is very limited, use giant sets.

These are only examples, and a way to say that there is always an option available! If your session won't be the exact same and won't be perfect, less is still better than nothing.

I think that too many people are too extreme. Obviously the goal is to respect your plan as much as possible, but also allowing space for the other things you love in your life. At least that is how I see it. Everything is about balance.

Doing less, and not nothing, participates in building your dedication and consistency up. Doing less is ok, as long as you are not quitting, and you keep on coming back to your initial programme.

However, you need to be honest to yourself and make sure you have a good reason to not have enough time to exercise. It cannot last for too long. If it does, you might then need to reconsider your goals as much as your expectations.

Life happens, unexpected things happen too. That should not be an excuse, but just a real taste of what can happen from time to time.

Create your Own Workout Programme.

13. STICK TO THE BASICS AND USE COMPOUND MOVEMENTS.

Stick to the basics.

The basics always work. In term of big muscle groups, using basic movements and their variations is more than enough!

If you are looking to improve your health, move pain free and feel better, using the basics will work perfectly for you. We are not talking about specific preparation here but general population health and wellbeing.

Stick to movement patterns explained in the very first chapter of this book, add consistency and progressive overload, whilst staying close to failure, and you can be sure that you will develop a great physical condition.

Exercises are probably the least important thing when it comes to programming. You first need to know what type of adaptation you'd like to create. Then make sure you are hitting all the patterns of movements to keep it balanced. Exercise selection comes after that. It might feel or sound very basic but basic is good.

Simple does not mean easy, the most challenging thing is to remain consistent. And once you manage to do that, you see real results.

Compound movements.

I am a big fan of compound movements! They hit lots of motor units, make you use different joints and different muscles.

They make you use lots of energy. If you want to be efficient, do not have lots of time to train and want to optimise your trainings, then using mostly compounds movements is a great idea.

However, do not get me wrong, using isolation exercises is good too. To emphasise some body parts you would like to focus on, especially at the end of your set or training, incorporating isolation movements can make a difference.

Add some isolation if you'd like to, or have extra time or extra energy.

Mix up the stress: isometric, eccentric, plyometric, explosive, maximum effort.

If there is a particular movement you'd like to improve or perform better, I'd recommend to place it as your main lift. If your goal is to improve your squat, then squat first! Later in the session you can work on accessory movements, understand hitting muscles that participate into the squat patterns (glutes, hamstrings, etc).

If you do not have any specific goal toward a specific movement, I'd suggest to start by the exercise in your session that will take most of your energy. Usually a leg exercise. If you are planning to deadlift today, probably start with it. Legs exercises require lots of energy and can be very tiring at the end of a session. If you want to make sure you perform well and make the most of it, placing it at the very start of your training sounds like the best option.

Your trainings don't always have to look the same. Mix up the supersets, the focuses, and the adaptations you want to create to keep them fresh and fun!

14. DO NOT OVERTHINK IT!

Sometimes, you might feel a lack of motivation when it is time to get changed and start exercise. The best advice I can give you is to get changed and exercise. Very often the most difficult part of exercising is getting ready and taking the decision of doing it. That happens to absolutely everyone, and that is the difference between motivation and consistency.

There are days where you will not want to train but still have to. That is how you get results. Obviously it all depends on your goals. If you just want a good sweat, fair enough.

However I am assuming that if you got this book, you probably have specific physical or even mental goals. Consistency will bring you where you want to be. It will take weeks, months if not years before working out becomes part of your life. It can take time to reach the point where you will treat resistance training as you treat brushing your teeth. That is to say, that it has become a habit that is vital to you, like eating or drinking water.

Enjoyable and doable.

Also, even though programming has its complex parts, there are 2 main rules you need to follow.

Your workout programme has to be enjoyable and doable! Let me explain.

It has to be enjoyable.

Like for the 80-20% rule that works for nutrition, I'd say that the same applies to training. You can't do only exercises you love, unless you love all of them, but you have to do mostly exercises that you love! That is the secret that will make you last.

If you find out about a new exercise that looks fun, and useful, put it in your programme. Do not wait until the end of your current one to try it out, if it is something that excites you. This is also why I recommend changing programmes every month, to keep it fresh and enjoyable.

Also, if you decided to focus on your legs this month, but that feels like too much after 2 weeks, mix it up. Nothing obliges you to go to the end. Do not get me wrong, you must still perform some legs exercises, but change your focus, or change the way you do it. You can switch a lunge for a single leg jump on a box. You can switch your extra chest exercises, which might be a dumbbell fly and go for some explosive push ups instead! Keep it fun and to your taste!

It has to be doable.

By doable, that means in the long term. There is absolutely no point wanting to exercise 5 times a week, if you know you won't sustain it in the long term. Instead, look at your schedule and find 1, 2 or 3 slots where you are sure you will be able to train. Your programme must fit into your life, not the opposite.

Doable also means at your level. You do not want to compare yourself to anyone else. This is a real challenge nowadays, with the impact of social media, but it is a very important point. Everyone is different and you have enough competitors with yourself. Challenge and focus on yourself only.

As a PT I know that including new fitness goals in your life can feel overwhelming. You might be reading different point of views and conflicting advice here and there. You might feel unable to achieve what you probably have been trying to achieve in the past. You might think it is not for you and have doubts. As a fitness enthusiast myself, I have the exact same thoughts and feelings. It is absolutely normal. Keep in mind that even though you may not like it at the start, your exercise programme needs to be more enjoyable than it is worrying or overwhelming. Understand that the thing that pushed you to start exercising and buy this book has to be stronger than the difficulty it takes you to keep up with your fitness. Remember that every time you worry or doubt. With consistency, days will become weeks and then months and years. Something that could feel difficult at the start will become easy and normal. Struggles will transform into healthy habits.

15. HOW TO MAKE SURE YOU IMPROVE.

This will be the shortest chapter of this book, but probably the most meaningful.

If you want to make sure you improve, follow these 9 rules.

The 9 steps to improvement.

Have a well-built programme.

That is to say, adapted to your lifestyle and your goal! Your training needs to be adapted to your life and not the opposite! If you want to last you have to have a programme that matches your life, something challenging enough but not overly so. Everything is about balance!

Keep track of your performance.

Weeks after weeks, months after months and years after years! It is a good way to follow your evolution, realise how far you have been, as well as monitoring your improvement! This is also massively helpful to build your new programmes! You can have a look at it and check how you used to perform and challenge yourself again!

Periodisation.

Fail to plan, plan to fail. You know the saying. Make a plan, follow the plan, and plan your own success.

Consistency.

This is key! There is no doubt that if your programme is good (and it will be now that you have read this book), and that you are consistent in your efforts (training and eating), YOU WILL HAVE RESULTS! Stay consistent! Even if the motivation is low, keep going! Less is better than nothing!

Progressive overload and deload.

Improve, rest and repeat. That is basically it. Work hard, increase the challenge, succeed and get well deserved rest. Then do it again. Consistency in efforts will lead you to constant improvement over time!

Stay close to failure.

That is the thin line between not training hard enough and training too hard. Your body can't handle going to failure all the time if you don't get enough rest. Push yourself often, not always. Rest and repeat. It is not easy to push yourself and you do not have to do it every session, sometimes a light session is much needed. Understand that if you never go to failure your results won't be optimal.

However, do not overwhelm yourself, there are days where you feel it and days where you don't. Build your habits first and learn how to trust yourself over time. Push yourself and go to failure when you feel like it, be consistent the rest of the time and you'll see great results.

Eat well: 80 – 20% rule.

No extreme is good. Balance is essential. You know I do not recommend cheat meals or cheat days. Eat different types of protein, carbs and fats. Some processed food is acceptable too. If you keep this ratio over the time, you'll learn how to manage your own weight.

Sleep enough and drink water.

This is very simple advice, but not easy to follow. This is probably the top 2 pieces of advice I would give to anyone feeling low, tired, stressed, or not in a great physical and mental state. Sleep 7 to 8 hrs per night and drink 2L of water. These are the very first steps to a healthier life.

Enjoy and have fun!

Learn to enjoy the process! After all, enjoying the journey is very important. Exercising is meant to be difficult and challenging. And that is because it's worth it. Only people that put it the work and the efforts can enjoy the benefits. You can move, make the most of your body and that is a privilege. Be aware of it! Move and love doing it!

Create your Own Workout Programme.

16. WORKOUT TEMPLATES.

Full body 1.

Session A	1. squats	2a. hinge SL	2b. push V SA	3. push H - plyometric	4. core or triceps
Sets	3-5	3-4	3-4	3-4	2-3
Reps	3-6	6-12	6-12	6-12	Time or 12-20
Rest	2-5m	45s	1m30	30s	90s-2m

Session B	1a. push V	1b. pull H SA	2a. push H SA	2b. pull V	3a. core	3b. carry
Sets	3-4	3-4	3-4	3-4	2-3	2-3
Reps	6-12	6-12	6-12	6-12	12-20 or time	Time or distance
Rest	45s	1m30	45s	1m30	45s	1m30

Session C	1. hinge	2. squat SL - jumps	3. pull V SA	4a. pull H	4b. core or triceps
Sets	3-5	3-6	3-4	3-4	2-3
Reps	3-6	4-6	6-12	6-12	Time or 12-20
Rest	2-5m	30s	90s-2m	45s	1m30

SL: single leg. **H:** horizontal.

SA: single arm. **M:** minutes.

V: vertical. **S**: seconds.

Create your Own Workout Programme.

Full body 2.

Session A	1. hinge	2a. squats SL	2b. push H	3a. pull H SA	3b. core or triceps
Sets	3-4	2-3	3-4	2-3	2-3
Reps	6-12	12-20	6-12	12-20	Time or 12-20
Rest	90s-2m	45s	1m30	45s	1m30

Session B	1. push V SA - plyometric	2a. pull V	2b. push H SA	3a. pull H	3b. carry
Sets	3-6	3-4	2-3	3-4	2-3
Reps	4-6	6-12	12-20	6-12	Time or distance
Rest	30s-45s	45s	1m30	45s	1m30

Session C	1. squat	2. hinge SL - jumps	3a. push V	3b. pull V SA	3c. core or biceps
Sets	3-4	3-6	3-4	2-3	2-3
Reps	6-12	4-6	6-12	12-20	Time or 12-20
Rest	90s-2m	30s-45s	45s	45s	2m

Full body 3.

Session A	1. push H SA	2a. squat	2b. hinge SL	3a. push V	3b. carry
Sets	3-5	3-4	2-3	3-4	2-3
Reps	3-6	6-12	12-20	6-12	Time or distance
Rest	2m-5m	45s	1m30	45s	1m30

Session B	1. squat SL - jumps	2a. push H	2b. push V SA	3a. pull H	3b. pull V SA	3c. core
Sets	3-6	3-4	2-3	3-4	3-4	2-3
Reps	4-6	6-12	12-20	6-12	6-12	Time or reps
Rest	30s-45s	45s	1m30	45s	45s	2m

Session C	1. pull V	2a. hinge	2b. squat SL	3a. pull H SA	3b. carry
Sets	3-5	3-4	2-3	3-4	2-3
Reps	3-6	6-12	12-20	6-12	Time or distance
Rest	2m-5m	45s	1m30	45s	1m30

Full body 4.

Session A	1. push V	2a. squats	2b. hinge SL	3a. push H SA	3b. core or biceps
Sets	3-5	3-4	2-3	3-4	3-4
Reps	3-6	6-12	12-20	6-12	Time or 6-12
Rest	2m-5m	45s	1m30	45s	1m30

Session B	1. squat - plyometric	2a. push V SA	2b. push H	3a. pull V	3b. pull H SA	3c. carry
Sets	3-6	3-4	2-3	3-4	3-4	2-3
Reps	4-6	6-12	12-20	6-12	6-12	Time or distance
Rest	30s-45s	45s	1m30	45s	45s	2m

Session C	1. pull H	2a. hinge	2b. squat SL	3a. pull V SA	3b. core or triceps
Sets	3-5	3-4	2-3	3-4	3-4
Reps	3-6	6-12	12-20	6-12	Time or 6-12
Rest	2m-5m	45s	1m30	45s	1m30

Create your Own Workout Programme.

17. EXERCICE BANK.

Examples of exercises.

Squat	Single Leg Squat	Hinge	Single Leg Hinge
Goblet squat	Lunges	Good morning squat	Single leg deadlift
Back squat	Walking lunges	Deadlift	Kick back
Front squat	Bulgarian split squat	Back extension	Exchanges
Spanish squat	Cossack lunges	Swing	

Vertical push	Horizontal push	Vertical pull	Horizontal pull
Military press	Chest press	Pull ups	Bent over row
Lateral raises	Push ups	Upright row	Monkey row
Landmine press		Y raises	Reverse fly
Jammer press		Lats pull down	

Carry
Farmer walk
Zercher walk
Rack walk
Mixed grip walk

Extension	Flexion	Rotation	Hips flexion
Plank and variations (instability, external tensions, weight)	Side plank and variations (instability, external tensions, weight) Single arm carries	Pallof and variations Chop and variations	Legs raises Knees raises Dead bug and variations (instability, external tensions, weight)

Create your Own Workout Programme.

18. ADVICE AND TIPS TO MAKE THE MOST OF THIS BOOK.

Last advice.

1. Alternate heavy and light weights on your supersets.
2. Change programme every month (keep it motivating & fresh). 1 week light, 3 weeks of progressive overloads and 1 week of maximum effort. Then start again by changing few exercises and focus.
3. You lose everything you don't work on, but you can't work on everything at the same time. Change your focus monthly: legs, pull, push, explosive etc.
4. Match exercise selection to save you time: use equipment that is close by or will be easy to use together in your gym (a good way to do that is to alternate barbells with body weight, or kettlebell with dumbbells, etc).
5. Balance your programmes from one month to the other. Ex: alternate core exercises, focus, push & pull etc. Best way to do that is to plan them in advance. There is no need to choose the exercises at that moment but deciding the frame and the focus is recommended.
6. Perform a minimum of 3 sets per exercise with one extra set to keep warming up.
7. Do unilateral work. Let me explain, just as you'd do squats with two legs, you can do a split stance squat. This works the same for the upper body. Barbell overhead press, dumbbell military press.
8. Work different muscle fibres and different ranges to be as complete as possible.

Create your Own Workout Programme.

19. THANKS.

Thank to you for taking the time to read this book! This means the world to me. I hope you found what you were looking for and that this book will help you achieve consistency and help you feel better, as much as it will be a guide to help you find your balance.

If you want to go further and learn more about health and fitness, are looking for more programmes or are interested in personal training, please visit:

equilibriumworkout.com

You can also follow me on Instagram:

@equilibriumworkout

Finally, if you'd like to, and I would very much appreciate it, you can also leave a comment or review on the platform where you got this book from.

Many thanks to you!

Kindly and healthily,

Jeremy.

20. ACKNOWLEDGMENTS.

This book would not have been possible without:

Sleep foundation.

Health line.

Why we sleep - Matthew Walker.

Jason Brown Coaching.

Secrets of Successful Program Design - Cosgrove and Rasmussen.

Caveman training.

Create your Own Workout Programme.

NOTES

Create your Own Workout Programme.

NOTES

Create your Own Workout Programme.

NOTES

Create your Own Workout Programme.

NOTES

NOTES

Create your Own Workout Programme.

NOTES

NOTES

Create your Own Workout Programme.

NOTES

NOTES

Create your Own Workout Programme.

NOTES

Printed in Great Britain
by Amazon